COAL CAMP MORNING
and OTHER POEMS

JASON KYLE RICHIE

COAL CAMP MORNING AND OTHER POEMS

iUniverse books may be ordered through booksellers or by contacting:

iUniverse
1663 Liberty Drive
Bloomington, IN 47403
www.iuniverse.com
844-349-9409

ISBN: 978-1-6632-1100-2 (sc)
ISBN: 978-1-6632-1099-9 (e)

Library of Congress Control Number: 2020919966

Print information available on the last page.

iUniverse rev. date: 10/09/2020

Foreword

It can be reasoned that Appalachia is a natural cradle for the qualities that make an author. Verdant old-growth forests draped in morning mist or the rugged beauty of craggy gorges certainly provide fertile ground for creativity. Nature's encompassing presence complements a rich—if sometimes dark—history. Unsurprisingly, both prose and poetry run deep into the culture of the Kentucky Coalfields. People of any culture struggle to capture their existence in words; we Appalachians are no exception, and poetry can be a particularly powerful vehicle to this end.

I am an educator by profession; poetry has simply become a treasured pastime in my life. In many ways, the following book is an author's journey. After suggestions from others, I decided to try my hand at publishing and hope readers will find enjoyment and perhaps the occasional thought-provoking moment in my work. Many of the following poems draw on the beauty of nature or the simpler facets of the human condition. Some are specifically linked to our culture, such as "Coal Camp Morning" or "The Clinchfield Train." "The Flood of '39" recounts the tragedy of the Frozen Creek Flood in Breathitt County in the summer of 1939. Others deal with history, Christian faith, the essence of seasons, and occasionally even biting satire. I feel that an author should not feel held down to a stereotype of the subjects that he or she writes about. Two of my personal favorites are "Essex Far Away" and "A Magnificent Desolation." These were inspired by the British retreat from Kabul in 1842 and the Apollo lunar program, respectively. "Heart of Vengeance," by contrast, is a social and spiritual critique set in the present with a potentially controversial subtext.

Both free verse and several rhyme schemes were used. My first real poetry effort was a nature poem inspired by a hiking trip called "A Fallen Leaf." I selected free verse for that poem, but I usually prefer the challenge of crafting a memorable rhyme. The poems in this volume were composed between December 2019 and July 2020.

J. K. Richie
August 2020

Dedicated to my friend and fellow amateur poet John Adkins for his encouragement to write and publish.

Contents

1. A Fallen Leaf

At the close of autumn,
a stillness falls in somber woods.
And on barren rock
lies a fallen leaf.
Crimson face to turquoise sky,
yet untrodden by the boots of men,
Soon to fade but not yet,
the leaf cast its final glory,
a transient beauty for perceptive eyes.

2. Firelight

I face the hearth at end of year;
crackling logs enchant my ear
in a cabin raised by stubborn might,
now bequeathed with Luna's light.
A refuge from self-doubt and fear,
kindling memories the heart hold dear.
Glowing hearth in darkest night
gives peace to one in firelight.

3. Sunrise

'Tis the time before the dawn,
as the night creeps ever on.
Stars glisten over snowy hills;
frost coats crystal on windowsills.
Then over the fog shines the light
of a vibrant sun in all its might,
to bid farewell to one winter night.

4. Bethlehem

On one darkened night,

there came one to give us light.

He came not for a worldly reign,

but instead to bear our pain.

On an earth filled with loss,

many burdens to shoulder on the cross.

As the angel choirs sing,

freedom did the Savior bring.

5. Time

Time is the ocean of boundless dreams,
the whirling current for our lives.
Regret may be a longing
for yesterday's tomorrow.
And hope is the catharsis
of days not yet come.
Yet it is time that carries all memories,
deep into the abyss of years.

6. The Trail

A path wound through emerald splendor,

ascended the timbered passes,

finding refuge beneath gnarled branches.

The trail passed blooming laurel,

wound straight stands of scented pine,

to cross the rock-strewn streams.

Along the summer trail I trod,

across the tracks of deer and bear,

to seek the joy the forest brings

to those walking in montane air.

7. The Flood of '39

Lightning arced across the sky
one night early in July.
Along the stream known as Frozen,
a tide came in as an ocean.
Before this tragic wall of fate,
the warnings came far too late.
With hope and tears did many pray
for all those lost by break of day.

8. Birth of a River

The morning was quiet,
the hills so forlorn.
Then a gushing of water
meant a river was born.
Through layers of time,
the water descended.
Illusions of permanence
the river upended.
Upon the fresh rapids,
sunlight did glisten.
And the river's roar sounded
to all who would listen.
In mountain and valley,
the birds did sing.
For life-giving water
would the river bring.

9. A New Year

The teapot's steam
and firelight's gleam
filled the cabin like a dream.
The time drew near,
a time so dear,
to bid farewell to yesteryear.
Ticktock chimed the clock
as ships of dreams depart their dock;
'tis time for a new year to unlock.

10. The Silent Night

Silent steps in careful flight,

seeking refuge from the night.

Through shadows of forest boughs,

silence yields to wolves' howls.

In the darkness,

Shawnee steel,

tomahawks drawn

for the kill.

Or the gleam of panther's eye,

in a quiet place in which to die.

The hunter dreads the forest night

when caught alone in pale moonlight.

11. In Light of Tomorrow

Wisps of steam danced
in flickering candlelight.
I sat there quiet with mug in hand,
my mind not yet contented.
My eyes but briefly peered
into the liquid coffee blackness
when I caught my own reflection.
Before me gazed a spark of hope
so far from prideful lies
or the schemes of vain ambition
to turn back this tide of depression.
Tomorrow was a new day,
a chance to seek the hope in us
and the peace of God's great blessings.

12. Wind

With a dry summer's burning,
or a winter storm's churning,
wind declares its returning.
Invisible, translucent, opaque,
even a gale with lives at stake,
the wind many forms may take.
On what forecast of wind,
does a good day depend,
or the plans of life bend?

13. From the Ashes

In kindling flame a forest dies,
burning beneath the reddening skies.
Fire crews worked with desperate might,
but against the inferno a losing fight.
When the sun rose on ash-laden hills,
a million charred trees our visage fills.
Yet from the hills, the ash will blow,
seeds will fall, and new life will grow.

14. Louisville Nights

Along the black Ohio wide,
the barges bring a gentle tide
as cars on bridges drive side by side.
And on these cold November nights,
I stroll beneath bright city lights,
my eyes delight in Louisville's sights.
Into the darkness the skyscrapers soar,
while high above the airplanes roar,
and city nights pass on before.

15. Morning at the Lake

Through gentle mist the light of dawn,
along the shore a doe and fawn.
Came God's creatures to the lake;
of life-giving waters they partake.
A crane perched on a half-sunk log,
a silent silhouette in lakeside fog.
Skipping rocks to pass the time,
an old mountaineer sings a rhyme.
Beneath the lake and unrevealed,
a sunken world the depths concealed.
With a lapping tide across the years,
the lake a place to cast out tears.

16. January

Snowflakes glide between the trees
as branches shiver in the breeze
and ice hangs perilously on the eaves.
Gray wisps of smoke from chimneys rise,
glowing embers fade in winter skies,
and ash the frigid wind rides.
Christmas is past, and January's here,
yet may we keep our loved ones dear
and pray God's love is ever near.

17. A Winter's Night

Across the fields of glistening white,
snow drifts like beacons in Luna's light,
the frigid visage of a winter's night.
The winds of winter at bay it may seem,
in warm homes where children dream,
or filled with coco's scented steam.
Old Man Winter has taken hold,
a snowy night will unfold,
and tales of winter will long be told.

18. The Ends of Time

Do I see time's end near,
or a reflection of misplaced fear?
Trust in the empire of the hour,
or have we faith in our Lord's power?
Some wait for a coming rapture,
longing for their souls' capture.
Others think the world is healed,
when the Great Commission is fulfilled.
Yet if Christ has opened heaven's gate,
why matters the course of fate?

19. Spring

Spring warms the weary heart in gardens of resplendent wonder.

Her flowers rise before our eyes,

colors upon life's canvas.

Bees whirl amid vibrant hues adorned in golden nectar.

And for those held down by winter's spell,

spring offers love most tender.

Dreary days be far behind for those who take her offer.

20. Clouds

Stretching out across the sky,
clouds so boundless and so high,
reside with those who dare to fly.
White, gray, black as night,
enrapturing beauty or twister's fright,
the clouds are a shifting sight.
Carried on an eastern wind,
in raging storm great trees bend,
yet clouds of tempest always end.
Clouds of night and clouds of day,
tranquil billows or storm on its way,
and clouds of dreams far away.

21. Kindness

Kindness glories not in prideful boasts,

nor does it stride indifferent to

those wearied by life's turns.

Kindness prefers to warm the dimming heart and takes upon itself the

thorny crown of another's burden.

Kindness is the triumph of simple right over intricate excuse. It is the

sum of a million lesser things coalescing to lift the human spirit.

22. Civil War

One's heart is at a loss
for a nation on its cross.
Bayonet fixed on Enfield's steel,
coldly driven to the kill.
But even with our towns aflame,
were our brothers all to blame?
Ram the charge into the bore
to cut them down with cannon's roar.
Then upon the field of the slain,
the agony of conscience pain.
Underneath the Stars and Bars,
never again yield to the demon Mars.

23. At Tomorrow's Shore

I stood on the shore of tomorrow
to watch yesterday recede.
Would another hour I borrow,
or would tomorrow my expectations exceed?
If adrift on the sea of years,
life's ship by swells overturned,
would I drown in the depth of fears,
or swim to shore with all I've learned?
For some, another hour is redundant,
and life's gift of time worthless.
But for others, a mere second is abundant,
and every tomorrow priceless.

24. Morning Coffee

On the ground where children play
came the first rays of dawning day.
With a click the doors unlock,
as outside the yellow buses dock.
To happy shouts the students enter
the halls they will long remember.
The teacher sips hot coffee steady;
for the school day she now is ready.

25. Mountain Sunset

At end of day the sun descends,

and in dying light its beauty sends.

With the sun setting low,

enchanted horizon with splendid glow.

Vibrant yellow and crimson red,

beauty has the sunset bled.

From our eyes the slipping light

as our view fills with night.

26. Honesty

Honesty can enter life uninvited
to rescue one from the slavery of vanity.
Though honesty may sear the coat of pride,
it can weld broken bonds of friendship.
Honesty steals the innocence of simplicity
yet bequeaths the treasure of truth.
Honesty cuts sharply with malice
but can be trust's lasting foundation.
Honesty lights a path through life
for those courageous enough to follow.

27. Storm Warning

A warning flashed upon my phone
of a storm tracked by weather drone.
Then fearful eyes beheld the storm,
though awestruck by its furious form.
With a visage dark as night,
sinister clouds eclipsed the light.
I soon beheld Old Glory torn,
a tattered flag in wind forlorn.
Lightning arced blue and white,
an electric dance with frightful might.
Sheets of rain filled the pail;
the rooftops echoed falling hail.
Then at last the wind died down
as the storm departed from town.

28. A Small Town

I want to see my small town thrive
when on its streets I take a drive.
Shops and trees line the way
as people pass the time of day.
I wonder what folks you'll meet
chatting on the old Main Street?
Perhaps as September rolls around
and time for the festivals to abound.
In city shadow the small towns lie,
but with much more than meets the eye.

29. "Empathy"

Empathy is the journey into another life,
a willingness to peer from other eyes.
Empathy restrains the excesses of logic
and is the leash of pragmatism.
Empathy lays the path for compassion
by bridging the gulf of divisive strife.
May empathy always be a companion
down the road God guides us.

30. Kentucky Stars

In the blackness of the night,
I stood enraptured by starlight.
Across millions of years
came the memory of distant spheres.
From the heart of stars that burned,
a light that time itself returned.
Stars can give us wonder
as our universe we ponder.

31. Friendship

A deep friendship is a symphony of the heart
composed by trust and devotion.
It rises to the resounding chorus of our joys
and endures sorrow with its own tragic beauty.
A false friend may back you in triumph yet leave you adrift when the
tides of fortune turn. A true friend, though, will share the burden of
your cross at each of life's hills called Calvary.
Friendship is a monument to love fashioned with the purest gold in
life's crucible.

32. The Right Side of History

When the last eye flutters shut
and the last word is spoken,
what becomes of the right side of history?
As the last monument weathers to dust
and the last written page crumbles,
what cause of man remains inscribed?
If one day the chorus of the streets ceases
and no hand remains to unfurl the flags,
can silence judge who was right or wrong?
Perhaps the vanity of every generation
is to imagine itself the apogee of history,
the zenith of civilization.
So beware seeking the legacy of the years
only to find a mocking indifference
reflected on the callous face of time.

33. Coal Camp Morning

A track meanders in mountain hollow,
along which the coal cars follow.
The coal camp sits in morning light
as families wake from the night.
Black coffee bubbles in the pot
as biscuits rise freshly hot.
A Model T drives up to the mill
laden with spirits from a copper still.
Along the road the miners talk,
as to the school their children walk.
Then beneath a wide chestnut tree
are memories of the past to see.

34. Apple Cider

A scent of apple and cinnamon
carried gently aloft, blending
in translucent clouds of steam.
For held fast in glazed ceramic,
a sweet pool of cider lay
as ambrosia for a winter's day.
Anticipating lips met the rim,
and warm, mahogany joy
flowed to delight the senses.

35. The Winter of '52

Eighteen years past his birth,
a boy entrenched in frozen earth.
Is someone there beyond the wire,
friend or foe—should he fire?
Then the gleam of ivory snow
basked in the transient flare's glow.
A silent prayer—all is well
for a moment in this frigid hell.
The only foe then was howling wind
on a Korean night watch nearing its end.

36. The Captain of His Fate

A boy gazed with restless eyes
pasts the masts in a northern fjord
to chart his course among the stars
as the captain of his destiny.
Past the years a clipper cut
through the swelling seas,
and with a smile at its helm,
the grown libertine.
Worlds then met in an ivory port
in the form of a refugee,
a thin, dark girl from the Ituri
with the eyes of destiny.
Under the bright expanse of stars,
lovers walked along an ancient shore.
And with a tide of freedom at their back,
a captain gave his love to destiny.
Then in years of failing health,
a dying captain wept at his legacy
of a virus spread from sea to sea
so he could be the captain of his destiny.

37. The Ohio River

The Ohio is a river of a thousand miles,
with a story to fill a myriad of files
coursing among the worn bridge piles.
With reed-strewn banks of silence found
and bustling stretches of city sound
and log jams where the waves pound.
Along the Ohio's murky flow,
perhaps a barge steady and slow,
or a river tug speeding to tow.
The river proceeds through our history,
carrying the gift of life's chemistry
yet enticing with depths of mystery.

38. The Simplest Things

Of all the moments that life brings,
may we treasure its simplest things.
A child's smile in a family game,
or a pet's greeting when in you came.
Vibrant flowers on a spring day,
or words of kindness that friends say.
Steaming coffee from the pot,
or a fawn grazing in the lot.
Remember the simple moments in the past
so in your memory their joy will last.

39. Fear

Sometimes fear keeps one from wrong,
but a different fear sings another song.
This fear lures us from the Father's light
and obscures the clarity of reason's sight.
Fear routes dreams to miss their mark
and snuffs out the light of creative spark.
Fear sets fire to the steeple
then turns its fury on other people.
May we keep watch for baseless fear
and keep the hope of courage near.

40. A Requiem for Utopia

The politicians promised to turn the page
so a socialist state could come of age.
But then the years went with a parting wail
as another system prepared to fail.
Even with loss, it wasn't the end,
for on no nation does life depend.
Promises cannot save a state
once incompetence decides its fate.

41. The One-Room School

The school stood by the old country store,
but except for memories, it stands no more.
Children once came by dawn's early light,
well-used books in their arms held tight.
A wood-fired stove provided the heat,
and beside it sat the best winter seat.
The school's first teacher was a disciplinarian,
but last year she died a centenarian.
Water was hauled from an adjacent stream,
the buckets now weightless in many a dream.
It's true the little school has no more learning,
but to its memories its students keep returning.

42. The Human Mind

A wondrous gift is the human mind
when curiosity finds compassion
and faith is aligned with reason.
Yet a mind may also be vindictive
or festering in paranoid delusions,
the slave of its unwise conclusions.
The mind, after all, is not simple,
but to the body like a temple
dedicated to the Savior's light
or lost in time to the night.

43. A Hiker's Prayer

Thank You for the beauty
in this place of solitude.
Thank You for fair weather
and a pleasant breeze.
Thank You for eyes to see
and ears to hear Your creation.
Father, please guide and protect me
in the forest that I love.
Please watch over those on the trail
and in their lives off it.
Please forgive us our sins in Jesus's name.
Amen.

44. Sinking of the *Monitor*

Clad in iron, she steamed to sea
just before New Year's of 1863.
Off Cape Hatteras the lightning flashed;
upon her armor great waves crashed.
Against the sea she was no match
as saltwater forced open a hatch.
The crew struggled with all their might,
but the ship was doomed that stormy night.
Those rescued would long remember
the fate of the *Monitor* that December.

45. The Foggy Night

As a translucent veil,
fog shrouds nocturnal hills.
Ghostly and ethereal,
its pale fingers creep
across the midnight world
to engulf all in gentle embrace.
Gleaming streams of light
soon pierce the milky current
as cars navigate treacherous roads
like ships on a darkened sea.
But high above this foggy night,
the moon and stars peer down
as if parents watching the world sleep
under a blanket of clouds.

46. To Ascend

Weary upon life's treacherous slopes,
I dug in tighter to faith's climbing ropes.
The path was long and the air getting thin,
but with joyful song I pressed onward to win.
Deep crevasses claimed many a hope,
but I blazed my trail with no time to mope.
I would not give in to steep depression's lie,
nor would I stop before I met the sky.
The summit I reached in exhausted pain,
ascending life's mountain a priceless gain.

47. By Lamp Light

The clock casts shadows at every tick
when in the glow of a lit lamp's wick.
From the radio came a soothing rhyme
while the wall clock's hands kept the time.
Outside the air is cold and damp,
but inside warmth with a glowing lamp.
Time to relax from life's dreary toil
beside the glass lamp's flaming oil.
How can a simple lamp contain such light
that comforts and consoles late at night?

48. A Coming Day

Have you seen the light
of a beautiful coming day?
It is a glorious sight
when your hope is far way.
May your mind forget
the burdens of regret.
'Tis time to reset
from the worries they beget.
Don't give in to the fear
or yield your self-esteem
to every rumor that you hear;
just let the coming day redeem.

49. Reflections on Regret

The sum of expectations never met,

little is as tragic as your regret.

When faith does not give the hope you lack,

regret is the apotheosis of looking back.

Give God the weight of your past,

and to your strengths hold dearly fast.

Try in life to be most kind

so to past mistakes you don't rewind.

Remember you cannot turn back time's clock,

but don't give regret the time to mock.

50. Reflections on Fear

Are you afraid of foreign lands
or simple germs on unwashed hands?
Do you fear eccentric people
or those under another steeple?
Do you fear a starless night
or the truth of heaven's light?
Do you fear the loss of those held dear
or the failing goals that seemed so near?
Will fear lead to your survival,
or will it halt the soul's revival?
Just be sure the danger is real
and not a reflection of hate you feel.

51. Bird of Prey

Above the quiet emerald fields,
an eagle descends in flight
as in its heart the tension builds
of the hunter's instinctual might.
Prey scurries about so far below
in the cold gaze of patient eyes.
Without a sound, they do not know
the wings on which fate flies.
Talons sharp as a peeling knife
descend from darkened wings,
for the raptor seeks another life
and the fullness that it brings.

52. Reflections on Respect

Respect demands from us a modicum of humility, a small sacrifice of petty ego for the greater good of civilization.

Conversely, a life without contemplating respect lacks an essential quality that helps complete the human person.

Respect does not imply the acceptance of wrong but extends a bridge of tranquility for those for those willing to cross.

53. The Bears

Resting quiet in its winter lair,
one finds the secretive black bear.
Then with spring's melting snow,
in forest glades the berries grow.
Ebony forms roam Appalachian hills
and feast uninvited in farmers' fields.
Hikers may spot their clawed tracks with fear,
but of people most bears steer very clear.
At times a danger the bears can be,
but a bear in the wild is a special sight to see.

54. The Face of Yesterday

Some wish for the world of yesterday,
and others to cast its memories away.

Some gaze upon our past in shame
while others bemoan what we became.

Our past was never Mayberry pure,
but every step forward was not a cure.

For people can see a different way
to perceive the face of yesterday.

55. Essex Far Away

No verdant fields are here to till,
just a lone, desolate windswept hill
and encircling Afghans closing to kill.
The India Company's best-laid plans
end with silent muskets in frozen hands
of soldiers' corpses in the Pashtun lands.
On the road from Kabul, the column lags,
scarlet targets for snipers in homespun rags
concealed behind boulders of lofty crags.
Past gray dawn of morning light,
on Gandamack Hill the final fight,
and no relief army was in sight;
command incompetence the soldiers' plight.

56. A Magnificent Desolation

Such blessed serenity to make one cry
on desolate mountains in an airless sky.
In gravity's dance with a familiar world,
along Earth's orbit with Luna hurled.
I bounded the craters as if in flight
beneath the stars of a lunar night.
On a desolate world without strife,
we stand humbled as its only life.
I thank the Creator for this momentous day
yet long to return to my world far away.

57. Chances

Friends suggest to give love a chance,
but every song is not your dance.
They warn the eyes tell many lies,
but strength to ignore them so often flies.
One may be accused of being too picky,
but to wait or not is often very tricky.
For it is easy to suggest love at a glance
when your own heart is not the one at chance.

58. Granny's Kitchen

Dumplings are cooking in the pot
with white chicken growing hot.
Granny, busy in her apron, cooks
as grandchildren give their hungry looks.
Green peas relax in steaming heat
before Granny calls the kids to eat.
Silverware adorns the family table,
ordered neatly as in a child's fable.
I return to Granny's kitchen in my mind
for few more pleasant memories I can find.

59. Ballad of the Sore Loser

He came to stroll the halls of power
fresh from his lofty ivory tower.
Yet doing no better than the rest,
he sought new fortunes in the West.
From his home out on the range,
he fought yet failed against the change.
When another hope for the party arose,
he struck a bitterly dissident pose.
While he calls himself a Latter Saint,
today he put on a coat of traitor's paint.

60. February

'Tis the second month of the year
when we best keep ready winter gear.
When February is warm, you'll be sneezing
before the next polar front sets you freezing.
Floods before snow may make you float,
but soon comes the shovel and a winter coat.
Soggy branches then bend to a wicked wind,
coating with slick ice that winter will send.
Our winter in Kentucky can be quite fickle,
so best have a humor that weather can tickle.

61. Traditions

Traditions are like a mirror
reflecting roads from which we came.
A passing of the torch
to light the paths of time.
Whether sportsman or scholar,
priest, peddler, or pauper,
traditions ask all of us
to reflect upon ourselves
with the light of all those
whose steps we follow
along life's journeys.

62. Language

Words upon a book's open page
inspiring joy or fomenting rage.
Language builds cultural bridges
and raises aloft dividing ridges.
Behold the power of the words we speak,
perhaps softly spoken but hardly weak.
Language can be a most helpful friend,
though on your words it will depend.
Write and speak with discerning thought
so in the path of fools you will not be caught.

63. When Rivers Rise

Inch by inch the rivers rise,
fed by the tears of sullen skies
eroding the permanence the land belies.
Refugees fled the rising flood,
swirling waters thick with mud,
a reddish brown like drying blood.
A flood submerges in the dark,
triumphant to its highest mark
to leave a landscape ravaged stark.
All this legacy of human pain
the mighty overthrow of worldly gain
was but the result of winter rain.

64. Numbers

Intangible, yet the fabric of all material reality
are the numbers we take for granted.
They are the symbolic representations
of men probing God's blueprints
for the nature of life and time.
Numbers are our keys of exploration
to the mysteries of worlds unknown.
They are like notes in a symphony
conducted with elegant synchronicity
on the wondrous page of the human mind.

65. The Blacksmith

Through cold dark of winter night
glowed the forge's flickering light.
With his hammer he pounds away,
working long from break of day.
Sparks ascend from every strike
shaping horseshoe or driving spike.
Bellows fan the white-hot flames
as iron ore the blacksmith tames.
Then the years came, and Bessemer too,
and now the blacksmiths are but few.

66. The Quilt Maker

A quilt of vibrant colors,
patched together with utmost care,
takes shape beneath a gentle smile
and the gaze of sky blue eyes.
In the prime of life, yet stressed
by the possibilities of a bustling world,
the quilt maker finds solace
in the tranquility of her hobby.
Her smile curves slightly upward,
mind at harmony with the still moment,
and hands diligently at her craft
to add one small beauty to the world.

67. The Misplaced Cynic

Some mistakenly see cynicism as
the edge of a sharpened mind
or the trusted path marked
by the sure compass of experience.
Yet cynicism is no true friend,
nor a marker of intellectual maturity,
but instead a weary surrender
to a simple view of life.
Life's reality is truly a summation
of tragic pain and beautiful joys
that cannot be encompassed
through a purely dim reference.

68. Testing Season

From the state a test is given,

And to new excellence are teachers driven.

To the test we swiftly run,

for the test is so much fun.

Embrace the test and clear your mind;

The state will not let you fall behind.

Students love to take the test,

So much better than all the rest.

So 'tis the season for the test,

And this season is the best.

69. The Swinging Bridge

An old man at night does often dream
of the old bridge across his mountain stream.
Planks of wood in the wind did sway
on that rickety bridge in years far away.
Many such bridges spanned those years
when money was tight in Depression fears.
But the gushing stream couldn't be leapt,
so moving forward one steadily kept.
The bridge finally went to the flood of '57,
and an old man wonders if such bridges be in heaven.

70. Trapped

Trapped in debt for all to see,
the student loans won't let him be.
Stress builds up from new assignments
for her to meet curriculum alignments.
Students stare blankly at their screens,
wondering what their effort really means.
Bank accounts dwindle for all the hours
while your youth the university devours.
Ask if liberal arts should be your hat
before you ask, "Do you want fries with that?"
College education should be reformed
so less lost time will ultimately be mourned.

71. The Hills in Splendor

From your youth, you may recall
the beauties of Appalachian fall.
Beneath skies so crisp and blue
are vibrant leaves of every hue.
The leaves glide softly in the wind,
so watch in admiration as they descend.
Blessed must be in the Creator's sight
Kentucky hills bathed in autumn light.

72. A Game in Time

Basketball is but a game we really know,
yet some moments the heart cannot let go.
Perhaps you remember the spring of '92
and a clash between teams of white and blue?
There were of course the referee decisions
and years full of counterfactual revisions.
But in the end, it was but a single ball
down the basket; our hearts would fall.
Many seasons and teams have went on by,
but for Kentucky fans, one game will never die.

73. A Furry Friend

A furry friend can warm the heart
when a kind owner does their part.
Though human words it cannot say,
it can show its affection anyway.
For many a blessing to watch them play,
in the joyful years with us they stay,
and bittersweet memories when they have gone away.
While its around, enjoy its presence,
and may you always remember a furry friend's essence.

74. Winter Passing

Have you felt your heart glow
at a leaf's shadow on winter snow?
Ascending slopes with tired knees,
yet mind refreshed by snow-laden trees.
To follow tracks, you may have chosen
reading a story that time has frozen.
Winter stillness can be so dear,
a refuge from the trials of the year.
To some, a burden are hiking packs,
but to many, a chance to relax.

75. The Lions of Njombe

Beneath the stars of the African night,
villagers in huts huddled in fright.
Predacious eyes watched the fields
as day by day the death tolls builds.
For many nights, the people would pray,
and finally a hunter came from far away.
With rifle in hand, Rushby stalked
the wilds of fear where many had balked.
And one by one, the lions fell
to free a land from their reigning hell.
For Njombe, it was a glorious day,
the end of a pride seeking human prey.

76. Reflections on Vanity

Do our eyes seek pleasure in reflection,
to be mocked by the mind's cruel rejection?
Has one gently come to offer her love
but left your gaze a wounded dove?
Do we know people are more than meets the eye, or do we cast them
aside for vanity's lie?
Must vanity reject our sins' remissions
and lure us into such futile ambitions?
Perhaps confidence, though, is really fine,
but be careful not to cross vanity's line.

77. A Sunday Morning

By the light of Sunday morn,
a new week is being born.
Through winter air so cold and still,
families ascending the chapel hill.
In a church anchored in faith's ground,
pews echo a glowing gospel sound.
Soaring like a graceful dove,
words proclaim the Father's love.
So thankful here at worship be
to praise Christ the Savior we are free.

78. The Polar Night

By the fire I huddle tight,
sipping coffee in its light
to the howl of wolves in polar night.
In the darkness, depriving sight,
lurk shadows of things that bite,
making myth of man's supposed might.
On tundra, no depth nor height
nor even snow shimmering bright,
just the visage of barren blight.
But beneath the aurora light,
I can say I feel all right,
safe and warm against the night
with my dreams taking flight.

79. The Clinchfield Train

Chugging along in Virginia fog
many long winters ago,
the Clinchfield train thundered into Kentucky lands destined for tons
of coal.
But a rockslide came and took her down
to the Russell Fork Breaks below.
Steam rose from the watery grave of the dying train as the sky wept
bitter snow.
But as years went by, the old-timers swear
a whistle still sounds in winter fog
from a ghost these mountains well know.
Perhaps be still and hear the haunting song
of the Clinchfield train wherever its journey goes.

80. The Forest's Edge

Before the silent stands of pine,
the bare boundary of wild wood
a demarcation of contrasting worlds:
industrial modernity raised by human hands
beside the primeval halls of nature's abode.
A wall of trees before my eyes,
rank upon rank of giants,
silent guards of their mysterious world,
enticing yet foreboding to curious eyes
at the shore of the forest abyss.

81. Depression

When depression's self-pity had seized me,
I pondered all the things I could never be.
Depression robs of joy and steals glee,
deceiving the very eyes from which we see.
Since happiness is depression's fee,
it often lies to us about reality.
So with depression do not agree
to allow it to darkly color what you see.
It will fight hard to get at thee
but struggle harder to make it flee.

82. Where Leopards Lie

Moon not risen in an Indian sky,
darkness conceals where leopards lie.
By day in fields, the farmers toil;
at night, paws track softly on the soil.
Mothers sing children lullabies
in homes watched by feline eyes.
Unsettling fear comes in the dark
when silence takes the guard dog's bark.
The door well latched, hope and pray
so the leopard does not find you as its prey.

83. A Wine Glass

A glass of wine can be a blessing,
but too much is quite depressing.
To some wine is most pretentious,
and to others drinking is licentious,
but a little be not unconscientious.
Wine can be relief to many a brother—
and the tragic downfall of many another.
Some prefer sweet, and some prefer dry.
Others unfortunately in drunkenness lie.
Red or white is but a preference,
but it's wise in amount to show deference.

84. Evening Coffee

Warm and fresh from the pot,
soothing aroma that delights a lot.
Whether simmering heat or frigid snow,
perhaps you simply need a cup of joe.
It judges not between rich and poor;
it will just ask you to pour some more.
While with friends discussing topics,
enjoy this pleasure of the tropics.
But if you need to catch up on sleep,
don't fill your cup quite so deep.

85. The Merchants of Fear

Should you meet the merchants of fear,
of their headlines keep very clear.
With more worry is a story sold;
sensational reporting never grows old.
The end is nigh, the end is near,
or so they say for the ends of fear.
Media statements grow ever more bold,
so on your mind their fear takes hold.
Our lives have their share of tears;
no need the burden of unwarranted fears.

86. The Merchants of War

Deep State deceivers clamoring for war,
proselytizing politicians pound on your door.
With slithering tongues to play on your fears,
they leave behind wrecked worlds of tears.
Endless excuses for an undeclared war,
never enough, always hungry for more.
Predators prowling on television screens,
the ends of power to justify their means.
It is not brave to send another to die,
but in power and profit do predators lie.

87. The Whirlwind

Woodward, Waco, and West Liberty too,
tornadic tragedies are old and new.
Bright Texas day or Nashville night,
sirens announce the whirlwind's might.
Silhouetted against the darkening sky,
the dreadful funnel churns ever nigh.
Pray not to seek mercy of furious winds
as homes from foundations it callously sends.
One may be awestruck at a tornado's power,
but please seek refuge in the whirlwind's hour.

88. Primavera, La Estacion de Bella

Mis ojos tienen deliste en tus maravillas

Mis oidos experimentan tus canciones.

Abajo el velo de tus nubes

un mundo es vivo en color.

Estoy gracioso por tus flores

y tus arboles en sus esplendores.

Ahora bailamos con nuestra Primavera bella

y celebramos el pasando de invierno oscuridad.

Spring, the Season of Beauty

My eyes have delight in your wonders,

my ears experience your songs.

Beneath the veil of your clouds,

a world is alive in color.

I am grateful for your flowers

and your trees in their splendors.

Now we dance with our beautiful spring

and celebrate the passing of winter darkness.

89. Anxiety

'Tis one thing to be a little shy,
but far worse is anxiety's lie.
You may miss your chance for love
or abandon talents like a wounded dove.
Anxiety whispers doubts into your mind,
so fight with courage to leave it far behind.
Emerge from the shadows of your past
and step boldly as God holds you fast
on a journey so long as your life will last.

90. The Last Stand

Life can be a daunting ride
to those who dare to buck its tide,
who take their stand on another side.
Futile at times may seem their song,
but they know when not to go along;
on tides of time they don't belong.
Lines drawn clearly in the sand,
feet planted firmly to take a stand
no matter the outcome of fate's hand.
Perhaps to the grave, perhaps to glory,
written in the wild wind is their story.

91. A Hunter's Morning

Before the misty morn of another morrow,
hunters are haunting hill and hollow.
In Kentucky fields where lambs wallow,
a grim trail do the hunters follow.
Hunters hunch with rifles ready,
barely breathing, sights so steady.
Coyotes cross the forest path,
longingly looking for what the herder hath.
A pack revealed in morning light,
exceedingly exposed, will never see this night.

92. The Erebus and the Terror

Leaving England on a favorable wind,
to the Northwest Passage they did intend.
Perhaps they served imperial schemes,
or perhaps the voyage of explorers' dreams.
But they met the white wastes of a frozen sea,
and an atrocious Arctic they could not flee.
Neither steam nor sail was of any use;
from the icy tomb they could not loose.
Hopes drowned when the ships went down,
and no survivors made the nearest town.
Franklin sought a new course to pave
but in the end found only an icy grave.

93. Yesterday's Town

When I find myself in a sentimental sway,
I may long to see the town of yesterday.
A Studebaker parked on a tree-lined street,
and the jukebox playing a familiar beat.
Perhaps further back, when the trains came by
while overhead mail planes would fly so high.
Then further in time, a rutted wagon street,
and old-timers tipping hats you would greet.
Back too far, and there were only trees
with mountain flowers welcoming bees.
Such a view is too romantic, I really know,
but the mind in dreams can enchant one so.

94. The Wait

Entering an era of contagious concern,

a hard road of patience we must surely learn.

For an invisible foe we, once vainly mocked,

now with regret has our attention locked.

This virus cannot love and cannot hate;

it is but a callous agent of natural fate.

But in God's strength and medical might,

with our newest foe we prepare to fight.

The road is not easy or always clear,

but a road we must take to conquer our fear.

95. Backroads

School buses carry most precious loads
along winding mountainous backroads.
The different classes live side by side,
sharing seats on the same bus ride.
In Appalachian fog and Kentucky rain,
the bus serves well though appearance plain.
Forested hillocks and roaring streams
race by passengers with future dreams.
Teachers wave to the buses passing by,
hoping students achieve dreams that fly.

96. A World Stood Still

Doors shutter and shop windows close
as news of the Wuhan virus ever grows;
a feeling of life halted everyone knows.
Silence grips a once bustling street;
handshakes forsaken when people greet,
if out about there is anyone to meet.
Uncertainty is a feeling most unkind
when orders and payments lag behind,
but to disruptions must we for now resign.

97. Por Los Estrellas

Como pinturas en tiempo
danado vivos a mundos,
Los Estrellas bailan
como diamantes en los cielos.
En la noche clara
son sus gloriosos revelado.
En las mas alla de enterplanatero
se llaman mid ojos.
Con los luces de los anos
se saludan todo mirran ascendente.

For the Stars
As paintings in time
giving life to worlds,
the stars dance
like diamonds in the heavens.
In the clear night
are your glories revealed.
In the great beyond of space,
you beckon my eyes.
With the light of years,
you greet all who look upward.

98. Running

Down the road across the creek,
day by day and week by week,
some in games may find their fun,
but with the wind I prefer to run.
My feet bounding to a steady pace
as a gentle breeze glides across my face,
such a refuge from internal strife.
I run for joy, I run for life.
Inside is not always a bad place to be,
but the world without has such sights to see
when with the wind running free.

99. Whispers in Time

Have you ever thought
of a quiet place in time?
A solace of the heart,
or a refuge for the mind?
In the deep abyss of stillness,
do you catch echoes of the soul?
And on the wings of dreams,
do you feel yourself in flight?
Is tranquility your companion
in the journey of your thoughts?
And in moments do you listen
for fleeting whispers out of time?

100. The Mine Called Number Five

In Kentucky hills course black veins of coal
where once was a mine the old-timers called
the Dreadful Number Five.
Like a dragon's mouth, the shaft went down
to a murky netherworld below; it struck one like the gates of
perdition when open in times of snow.
The miners for years lit their lamps and shouldered picks to toil in
depths where coal seams grow.
In all that time, the Number Five made its fortunes and made its
graves for those souls seeking black gold.
But then one day the beams gave in, and for one mine, it was the end
save for the stories
told round the mining camp hearths for many long years to come.
Perhaps you've heard of the old Number Five, where so many brave
lads on their last day would go.

101. The Age of Sail

Her masts like clouds above the sea,
bow crashing through waves wild and free;
a piece of your heart is the ship to thee.
To what distant isle will you now head
when chart and compass you have read,
or following silent stars wherever they led?
Neither pirate nor tempest stifles your heart,
and from your course you will not depart
until all the discovery to posterity you impart.

102. The Burden

It seems in life, no matter what we gain,
a heavy burden is the reality of pain.
Some say pain is the consequence of sin,
a fall that our choices have put us all in.
Others argue it is not from antipathy,
just the mechanics of nature's apathy.
Or is our suffering predestined fate
constructing a plan mysteriously great?
I believe in the Creator and in His cross,
but to discern pain, I am frequently at a loss.

103. The Machine

Have you seen the latest automation today?
Has his presence kept your fears at bay
with soothing words your mind to sway?
It is fine to commend a competent job,
but I fear the calls of messiah from the mob,
for precious freedoms machines may rob.
Much given to keep others from the tomb,
yet factories stay open to kill in the womb,
and the ironies of life over our heads do loom.
In moments of crisis, disagreements on hold,
but when it is past, don't find yourself sold,
for the story of human nature never grows old.
This crisis will pass as all such to date,
but beware of remaining the eyes of the state,
or cogs in its machine may be our fate.

104. To Find Tomorrow

Forever in darkness the world may seem,
but for careful eyes, a new dawn's gleam.
Pestilence and panic beset the mind,
but in tomorrow's light is new hope to find.
As billowing waves in the sea of time,
trouble's wax and wane is a familiar rhyme.
This for many may be a time of sorrow,
but even pain runs out of time to borrow.
Hope in darkness seems unimaginably far,
yet below the horizon is a heavenly star.

105. Resurrection

An April dawn in a world of strife
lit an empty tomb heralding life.
Days before, a man bore the load,
facing humanity at its cruel crossroad.
The incarnation of God on Earth
risen to show us our possible new birth.
Though centuries ago in the time of Rome,
His presence through time fills many a tome.
So if Christ lays out a better way,
will we let Him guide us this very day
toward the eternal home of which He did say?

106. The Steadfast Heart

Should we not seek a steadfast heart
knowing pretensions of grandeur invariably depart?
For no lust for pleasure nor thirst for gain
can dare halt life's inexorable wane.
Mortality awaits with a tragic smile
dismissive of rank and apathetic to guile.
So stoic in heart the wise should be,
for the fabulous frailty of life they see.
Vanities of power and passionate greed
should burn on the pyre of a higher creed.

107. Compass

Past failures recede to a quickening stride
for to every season there is a time.
To forlorn regrets do not resign,
but to love's compass your heart align.
Well worth a voyage across your fears,
occasional tempest with tides of tears,
for love's refuge awaits down through the years.

108. Utopia

Work makes free,
the sign clearly read,
a lullaby in iron
for the walking dead.

'Tis the end of history,
a theorist once said,
as a dragon rose quietly
upon an Eastern bed.

We're in this together,
the daily jester pled.
For life is so precious
until we take it instead.

And down the roads to Utopia
the masses were led,
where loyalty is honor,
Big Brother's offerings blood red.

109. A Lonely Soul in Time

Have you ever met such a lonely soul in time
renouncing tender mercies for the thrill of freedom's lies?

Enslaved by false hopes on the wings of desire,
can one chained to the moment seek rest in something higher?

Resenting all he richly has at the beckon of his pride,
will he ever find fulfillment short of laying down his life?

110. Heart of Vengeance

On the road to retribution, do you ever gaze within
to a visage of the soul, gaunt and pale from sin,
struggling in a race that no man alone could ever win?

And if your brother's life so matters,
why hangs he on your cross,
unless your chanting was but chatter,
and his pain to you no loss?

Have you shed tears vainly for things you've never done
while wasting in vapidity the time God gave you in the sun?

On rising tides of anger, do you cast aside the law,
proudly condescending from a soapbox, mighty tall,
unaware your perilous stance leads only to a fall?

From the eyes of God, our wrath we cannot hide,
walking hand in hand with vengeance so gladly at our side,
letting sanity slip away while we slowly die inside.

111. A Summer's Night

The delicate veil of Luna's light
may envelop the heart on a summer's night,
while a whispering wind through dark branches above
guides a young couple on a journey of love.
Fireflies frolic over grass emerald green
like lanterns lighting from darkness now seen
in a forest alive round a placid coursing stream,
and embers cool where tired campers dream.
So relax for a moment on this summer night;
with the Lord above will you be all right
to find a moment of peace beneath a canopy of starlight.

Printed in the United States
By Bookmasters